Who is Go

What Muslims Believe

Allah Is One
The absolute oneness of Allah is primary to Muslims. The greatest sin is to associate any partner with him. This sin is called *shirk*. Muhammad's message advocating one God was courageous because idolatry was the established religion of Arabia. Muhammad challenged this system and finally prevailed with the message of monotheism. Islam is rooted in this commitment to the belief in one God.

Allah Cannot Be Compared
Allah is transcendent and cannot be compared to humans or any other created thing. Allah's character and attributes are revealed through his 99 Arabic names, the two most common being "The Merciful" and "The Compassionate." Allah is never described in Islam by using human family terms such as "father" or "son." In the Quran he reveals his will for mankind to obey, not his person for mankind to relate with and know.

Allah's Ultimate Attribute: His Will
Allah creates and sustains all life, spiritual and material. His will is absolute and cannot be questioned by his creation. He is our final judge without a mediator. The best chance on Judgment Day is for those who live lives of righteousness and submission to Allah's will—*Insha Allah* (God willing).

What Christians Believe

God: A Unity, Not a Unit
The Bible teaches that God is one, but he is a complex unity, not just a simple unit. He is completely unique, a personal God who existed in relationship from eternity.

God the Father, God the Son, God the Holy Spirit
Scripture reveals God as the ultimate Father, in name, character, and person, but always as the Creator, never with sexual references. God also reveals himself as the Eternal Word, who became flesh when the Holy Spirit overshadowed the Virgin Mary and conceived Jesus, the Messiah, who is also called the Son of God in the Bible. In his teaching, Jesus further reveals God the Holy Spirit, who was sent by the Father and himself.

The Bible p… mystery of three persons revealed as one God. Although the word "Trinity" is not in the Bible, the term captures Bible truths about God. The Father, the Son, and the Holy Spirit are God, not just three parts of God or three names for the same person. God reveals himself as a tri-unity.

God's Ultimate Attribute: His Love
The Bible says, "God is Love." This love existed from eternity as the Father loved the Son even before the foundation of the world. God's love is expressed through creation. God does not simply choose to love; his love chooses to act. "God so loved the world that he gave his one and only Son" (John 3:16).

How to Correct Misunderstandings

The Misunderstandings
Most Muslims consider Christians to be polytheists (people who believe in many gods) because of the Trinity. A popular misunderstanding of the Trinity is that Christians believe that a Father God had sex with a Mother God (Mary) to produce their "Son of God." No Christian believes this. Educated Muslims understand this false Trinity is not what Christians believe, but they still do not understand how the math can show God's unity. To them it is simple: 1+1+1=3; Father + Son + Holy Spirit = Three Gods. This is not what Christians believe.

Correcting the Misunderstandings
Rather than use an analogy of adding units (1+1+1=3), the Trinity has been explained as multiplied wholeness (1x1x1=1). The Bible says Jesus is the eternal "Word of God" revealed in flesh through the virgin birth. The Quran sets apart Jesus as "His (God's) Word" and "a Spirit from Him (God)" and mentions his virgin birth and miracles. Muslims also believe in the second coming of Jesus, because Jesus is called the "Sign of the Hour" in the Quran. Muslims like to point out how the Quran honors Jesus. Yet such positive references to Jesus in the Quran are few compared to the complete story of Jesus preserved by God in the New Testament.

Notes and References

Allah The proper pre-Islamic Arabic name for God, used even today by Arabic-speaking Christians as well as by Muslims. Scholars think the word "Allah" is originally a compound of *al-ilah* ("the god"). Although all Muslims use the Arabic name "Allah," only 20% are native Arabic speakers. Muslims with other native languages have still another name for God. For example, Farsi-speaking peoples use "Khodah" to mean God. Bible translators usually employ the native language term for God, the uncreated Creator.

Muslim An Arabic term derived from the same root as the word for peace (*salam*). Note that the trilateral root _S_L_M_ is shared by all these related terms: **SALAM**, **ISLAM**, MU**SLIM**. The root and its derivatives are very similar to the Hebrew word "Shalom," which means peace.

Baraka Literally means "blessing," a term that communicates well to Muslims. Baraka is a central biblical theme first introduced by God to Abraham (*Ibrahim*) in Genesis 12:1–3, and extended to all believers of all nations (Gal. 3:6–9).

Pillars The five pillars of religion (*arkan-ad-din* in Arabic) are referred to by their Arabic names by all Muslims, regardless of their native language.

- **Confessing the Faith** (*Shahada*) is a public statement said in Arabic which means, "There is no God but Allah and Muhammad is His Messenger." Making this confession is the first step in becoming a Muslim. Islam requires that everyone say this confession in Arabic.
- **Prayer** (*Salat*) is a set ritual to be done five specific times every day (sometimes combined in three sessions), memorized in Arabic, with ritual washings before each sequence. The head must be covered, the body pointed in the direction of Mecca, and the motions and prostrations must be followed for the prayers to be valid.
- **Fasting** (*Sawm*) is an annual community event for all Muslims (except children, pregnant women, and travelers). The fast lasts the entire lunar month known as Ramadan, and involves abstinence from all food, water, and sex during daylight hours. At sunset, when the daily fast ends, there is a special meal (*iftar*) and another just before sunrise. In Muslim dominated countries there is often a shift to a more nocturnal schedule with more sleep during the daytime and feasting at night.
- **Giving of Alms** (*Zakat*) is obligatory giving of 2.5% of a Muslim's wealth, primarily to the poor and for the support of religious and educational institutions or the self-defense of the Islamic community.
- **Pilgrimage to Mecca** (*Hajj*) is to be carried out at least once in a lifetime, providing a Muslim can afford it. Uniformity is enforced in the manner of dressing—in a white garment—to shaving the head (for the men). The objective is to strengthen Arabic-Abrahamic identity by recalling the story of Hagar and Ishmael and the union of all Muslims by circulating around the ancient Arabic-Abrahamic religious center (*Kaaba*). Great claims are made for gaining multiplied credits as well as removing the weight of sins in preparation of the scale of Judgment Day.

Featured Photos and Artwork

Ring (page 2): Afghanistan is famous for its dark blue lapis lazuli gemstone, set here in a hand-crafted silver ring featuring a clear symbol of the Trinity. Although its meaning may be lost in this Muslim nation, this is an ancient Christian symbol of Tri-unity and eternity.

Arabic translations of the Injil (Gospel of Luke) and Taurat (Genesis) (page 3): Muslims treat holy books with great respect, putting them on special reading stands and some wrap them in protective cloths.

Muhammad and the Archangel Gabriel (page 4): Copy of a sixteenth-century Turkish manuscript called *The Progress of the Prophet*. Notice the prophet is veiled to avoid sacrilege.

The Kaaba (page 5): The Kaaba is a cube-shaped building in Mecca toward which Muslims pray. Muslims believe the Kaaba was an altar used by *Ibrahim* (Abraham)

Time magazine cover and advertisement (page 9): This magazine cover and advertisement on the back display a common misunderstanding about Western culture.

Compares Basic Teachings and Beliefs

Islam & Christianity

- Reaching Out to Muslims
- Answering Misunderstandings

ROSE PUBLISHING

Religious History

What Muslims Believe

Islam, the Original Religion
Muslims believe that Islam (meaning "submission" to Allah) is the original religion since the creation of Adam, the first prophet. Since the beginning of time, all people who submit to Allah are called Muslims. Over the centuries, Allah appointed thousands of prophets to warn and guide mankind. Prominent among them were *Ibrahim* (Abraham), *Musa* (Moses), *Dawud* (David), and *Isa Al Masih* (Jesus the Messiah).

Muhammad, the Final Prophet
Mankind habitually strayed from the way of Allah revealed through the prophets. About AD 610 in Arabia, Allah sent the last prophet, Muhammad, who united the Arab tribes and turned them from idolatry to Islam.

The Spread of Islam
After the death of Muhammad in AD 632, Sunni Islam rapidly spread from Arabia under the leadership of the first four "rightly guided" rulers (*caliphs*) who were close companions of Muhammad. Shia Islam began to rapidly spread through the teachings of "infallible" Imams from the bloodline of Muhammad. To Muslims, the military and economic expansion of Islam liberated people suffering under the corrupt Byzantine and Persian Empires.

What Christians Believe

Adam and Jesus
Christians also trace their religious history back to Adam, who brought the curse of sin upon all mankind (Gen. 1–3). In the Bible, Jesus is known as the second Adam, who came to remove this curse of sin (Rom. 5).

Abraham and Jesus
God's plan unfolded carefully over history. Abraham (*Ibrahim* in Arabic) was promised the blessing to carry out God's eternal purposes. He was blessed so he could be a blessing to all the families of the earth (Gen. 12:1–3; Gal. 3). Jesus is the promised seed of Eve who would crush the head of Satan (*Shaytan* in Arabic; Gen. 3:15) and bring the blessing of the "Good News" (*Injil* in Arabic).

The Victory of Jesus
A great war has been raging throughout the Creation, a struggle in which Satan has twisted all good things—even religion—into weapons to discredit God. The decisive battle of this war was won on the cross when Jesus destroyed Satan's power and overcame the curse of sin. By rising from the dead, Jesus conquered death, a consequence of the curse, and thereby offers the blessing of eternal life to mankind.

How to Correct Misunderstandings

The Misunderstandings
Religious history between Christians and Muslims is covered with blood and war, much like all of human history. God's name has been used by both sides to justify murder and mayhem. Several key events in history continue to affect the perceptions of Christians and Muslims. These events include the Islamic expansion (7th–8th centuries), the Crusades (11th–13th centuries), the establishment of the state of Israel in 1948, the attack on the World Trade Center, the Gulf Wars of 1991 and 2003, and many other events.

Correcting the Misunderstandings
Historians have pointed out that these "holy wars" of history were more about economics than faith. Yet economic struggle cannot explain the intense hatred, cruelty and malicious evil of a Crusader, Nazi, or suicide bomber. Behind these horrors is a deeper spiritual war and a vindictive enemy, namely Satan. Christians and Muslims should not lose sight of Satan, the "enemy of souls." By recognizing the common enemy, Christians can create a context in which they can build relationships with Muslims.

Helpful Words and Terms

Although 80% of Muslims do not converse in Arabic, all Muslims use some Arabic terms and phrases because Islam requires uniformity. For example, the Arabic names of all their prophets, including Jesus Christ, are easily recognized by Muslims. The same is true with the universal Muslim greeting, "Salaam alaykum," because Muhammad required it to be used. For a Christian to use some Muslim-friendly words can help avoid misunderstandings, but it can also lead to the impression that one is interested in converting to Islam. This is a risk worth taking in order to communicate the Good News as a truly positive message, not as a corrupting influence. The following phrases and terms are among the most helpful in using with Muslims. It is good to ask your Muslim friend to help you pronounce these Arabic terms.

Bismillah (Bis-mi-LAH)—"In the name of Allah." An invocation frequently used by Muslims. The longer version, Bismillah ar-Rahman ar-Rahim, means "in the name of Allah, the Compassionate, the Merciful." As a way to honor their Muslim friends, Christians can ask for help to memorize and appropriately speak this Arabic phrase because similar terms are deeply rooted in biblical understanding.

Hadith (Hah-DEETH)—Thousands of reports of sayings or behaviors of Muhammad which set a precedent for Muslim practice and becomes the basis of Sharia law.

Ibrahim (E-brah-HEEM)—"Abraham"

Injil (In-JEEL)—Refers to the "book given to Jesus" and comes from the Greek word *evangelion*, meaning "good news." Muslims do not believe that there is an Injil remaining on the earth that has not been corrupted. Christians often refer to the Gospels or a single Gospel as "the Injil" when conversing with Muslims.

Insha Allah (In-SHA-al-lah)—"God willing." This common phrase is often tagged onto a sentence expressing hope or intention, and sometimes resignation to destiny. It is an expression of Allah's ultimate attribute: his absolute will.

Isa Al Masih (EE-saw-all-Mah-SEE)—"Jesus the Mes-si-ah." The word "Ma-sih" is similar to the Hebrew word. "Isa" for "Jesus" is an obscure version of the Arab Christians' *Yasu* (from Hebrew *Yeshua*).

Salaam Alaykum (Sa-LAAM Ah-LAY-kum)—"Peace be upon you." It is virtually identical to the Aramaic phrase Jesus spoke when appearing to the disciples after his resurrection (Luke 24:36; John 20:19).

Sharia (Sha-REE-ah)—"Path to water." Islamic religious and civil law which is based upon the Sunna, Quran, and Hadith. Sharia is a guide to everyday life and salvation. Sunni scholars developed four schools of interpretation named after their founders: Hanafi (d. 767), Maliki (d. 795), Shafii (d. 820), and Hanbali (d. 855). Shia have their own similar schools.

Shaytan (Satan) (Shay-TAAN)—An evil *Jinn* (fire-born spirits in Arabic folklore), not a rebellious angel. The Quran uses this term to refer to mischievous behavior (like devilish).

Shiite or Shia (SHE-ite or SHE-ah)—"The party of Ali" (10% worldwide) that believes that the proper successor to Muhammad should be his blood relative, beginning with Ali. The Sunni-Shia split happened shortly after Muhammad's death in a violent dispute about who should lead the Muslim community.

Shirk (SHIRK)—"Associating." Idolatry or blasphemy. Making others equal to God, an unpardonable sin, like disbelief (*qufr*).

Sufi (SOO-fee)—Muslim mystics, who can be either Sunni or Shia, range from storytellers seeking to love Allah and his wisdom to those inducing trances through chanting the names of Allah or dancing (as seen in "whirling dervishes").

Sunna (SOO-nah)—"Trodden path" of Muhammad and his close companions. The Sunna (Muhammad's examples) becomes the basis of Sharia law.

Sunni (SOO-nee)—"One on the path;" how the majority of Muslims (90% worldwide) identify themselves as contrasted to Shiite.

Taurat of Musa (Tor-AT MOO-sah)—"Torah of Moses," the book given to Moses. The first five books of the Bible.

Tawheed (Toe-HEED) "Oneness." A term used to refer to the absolute oneness of Allah.

Zabur of Dawud (Zah-BOOR DAU-ood)—"Psalms of David," the book given to David, the Psalms.

Holy Scriptures

What Muslims Believe

The Only Trustworthy Scripture
According to Muslims, there is only one trustworthy Holy Scripture, the Quran ("a text to recite"). Many prophets before Muhammad were also given Allah's Word, among them: *Musa* (Moses) given the *Taurat* (Torah), *Dawud* (David) given the *Zabur* (Psalms), and *Isa* (Jesus) given the *Injil* (Gospel). However, Muslims are taught that all these writings were corrupted. Allah appointed Muhammad to receive the Quran in order to correct this corruption.

How Muslims Got the Quran
In AD 610, Allah sent the archangel Gabriel (*Jibrail* in Arabic) to Muhammad in Mecca, Saudi Arabia. Over the next 22 years, Allah "sent down" revelations to Gabriel who dictated them to Muhammad with the command to recite it to others. Shortly after Muhammad's death in AD 632, his followers gathered the texts of different lengths into 114 chapters (*Sura* in Arabic). The third caliph, Uthman, had scholars compile an official Quran, in written form, and had all other variant texts burned.

The Quran Today
The Quran is considered divine in its original Arabic form, and Muslims memorize and recite it only in this pure language.

What Christians Believe

How Christians Got the Bible
Followers of Jesus believe the Bible is the authoritative, inspired word of God, composed of 66 different books, transmitted through at least 40 prophets, apostles, and holy men. The first 39 books, written before the coming of Christ, are called the Old Testament. The Old Testament was written over many centuries by various authors in diverse cultures using the Hebrew and Aramaic languages. The remaining 27 books after Christ are called the New Testament. They were written in Greek, the dominant language of the 1st century. The New Testament contains collections of eyewitness reports of the life and teachings of Jesus, followed by a history of his disciples over the next 50 years, including letters from his apostles and a vision of the end times called the "Revelation."

Inspiration
The Christian view of inspiration is that God "breathed" his Word through many people (mostly inspiring, rarely dictating). Therefore the Bible reflects cultures as diverse as Abraham's nomadic lifestyle to the royal court of King David. The result is a book of beautiful human diversity interwoven with divine unity.

How to Correct Misunderstandings

The Misunderstandings
Muslims feel sorry that Christians follow a corrupted book and most Muslims avoid the Bible. Even among Western-educated Muslims, the great diversity of Bible versions and translations adds to their belief that the Bible is corrupted.

Correcting the Misunderstandings
Muhammad did not question the accuracy of the Bible; he criticized contemporary Jews and Christians for misinterpreting or not obeying their existing Scriptures. The accusation that the text of the Bible had been corrupted came centuries after Muhammad, at a time when Muslim scholars realized there were contradictions between the Quran and the Bible. Yet the Quran points to the Bible as truth to obey many times. The text of the Bible is better preserved than the writings of any ancient author. Furthermore, the discovery of the Dead Sea Scrolls confirmed the reliability of the Bible.

Religion and Culture

What Muslims Believe

The Muslim Holistic Worldview
Muslims understand religion as a whole and integrated way of life. Secular, Christian-influenced cultures can confuse and even anger Muslims who see things through their holistic worldview. They often view "Hollywood sexuality" as "Christian," or a military action as a "Crusade." To them, the cross is a military symbol.

The Islamic Community
In Islam, brotherhood and consensus is emphasized, and individualism is avoided. The "community of the faithful" is responsible to enforce the moral code. This can explain how a lone Muslim, outside a community support structure, does not feel as guilty when breaking the code. However, bringing shame on his family or community would be a great sin.

Avoiding shame and protecting honor are primary motivations of most Muslims. Shame and honor are community-related, as contrasted to an individual sense of guilt.

Radical Muslims, known as Islamists or Jihadists, use this sense of community honor and shame to recruit and motivate their followers.

What Christians Believe

The Western Worldview
Followers of Jesus believe that they are to impact culture for Christ by going into all parts of the world to bring the message of Jesus to the people that live there (Matt. 28:19–20). In the West, a division exists between culture and religion. Religion is separated from government, and some people object to any influence of religion on state institutions and symbols.

Community in the West
Followers of Jesus do influence Western culture and institutions, but they seem to be a shrinking influence. Western culture affirms individualism and some people avoid community responsibility. Tolerance of sin and unbiblical practices continue to dilute the true Christian message; evolutionism and atheism also continue to influence the increasingly secular West. Only a minority of those in the West consider themselves followers of Jesus Christ. Most simply consider themselves Christian by name only, and do not follow the teaching of the Bible, of which they are largely ignorant. Generally, Western culture does not have a sense of the "community of the faithful."

How to Correct Misunderstandings

The Misunderstandings
Time magazine ran a cover article asking the question, "Should Christians Convert Muslims?" The artwork featured a militant-looking clenched fist holding a metal cross, reminiscent of a Crusader's sword. This imagery correctly symbolizes some typical Muslim misunderstandings, especially when viewed with the cigarette advertisement on the back cover. The advertisement features a sensual goddess-like model with men fawning at her feet. These pictures display some fears of Muslims: to be dominated militarily and corrupted morally by "Christianity."

Correcting the Misunderstandings
The challenge is to present a correct view of the cross. The movie, "The Passion of the Christ," has been seen by Muslims all over the world. They have seen the cross as a symbol of suffering, not as a military or political icon. Followers of Jesus, through their words and actions, are called to show Muslims that God loves all people so much that Jesus died on the cross for their sins. (Islam denies Jesus' death; claims that he was lifted up to heaven and a substitute died instead of him.) Jesus also defeated Satan and death by rising from the grave. He made it possible for all of God's children to live with him forever. This "good news" should be attractive to Muslims.

Prophets

What Muslims Believe

Muhammad, the Seal of the Prophets
To Muslims, the Prophet Muhammad, called the "seal of the prophets," is the last of over 124,000 prophets going back to Adam. His name means "praised one," and he is commended by Allah in the Quran.

Muhammad, the Reformer
Mecca was a center of idol worship in AD 610 when Muhammad first challenged the people to forsake idolatry and embrace Islam. Most Meccans rejected his message and many began to persecute the early Muslims, causing them to flee to the town of Medina in AD 622. (This flight is known as the *hijara* and marked the first year on the Islamic calendar.) Medina was more receptive to Muhammad, and from this city, through battles and diplomacy, Islam was spread to the entire Arabian Peninsula within only a few years after Muhammad's death in AD 632.

Muhammad, the Perfect Example to Follow
Muslims try to follow Muhammad's example known as his *sunna* ("trodden path" or "customs") in every detail possible. Everything is prescribed, from ritual washings before prayer to hygienic practices in the bathroom. Such detailed behavior is known through large collections of *hadith*, accounts of Muhammad's life, words, and behavior passed on by his early followers.

What Christians Believe

Old Testament Prophecy
New Testament writers proclaimed Jesus as the fulfillment of the Law of Moses (*Taurat*) and the predictions of Old Testament prophets. These prophets are quoted in the New Testament. For instance, Matthew quotes various prophets concerning Jesus' birth in Bethlehem (Mic. 5:2), his mother being a virgin (Isa. 7:14), and even the killing of baby boys by King Herod (Jer. 31:15). The prophets also detail the suffering, death, and resurrection of Jesus (Isa. 53; Ps. 16:8–11). The Bible points out that God carefully planned and carried out the details of the coming of Jesus in history (Luke 24:27; Acts 3:18).

Christ's Warning about False Teachers
The Bible contains numerous warnings about false teachers and prophets. Jesus predicts the end times will be full of these (Matt. 24: 11). Therefore, every teaching must be judged against the truth already revealed in the Bible. Jesus also promised that the Holy Spirit ("the Spirit of Truth") would guide truth seekers into all truth (John 14–16).

How to Correct Misunderstandings

The Misunderstandings
In conversation with Muslims, do not attack Muhammad. Since so much is determined by imitating their prophet, to insult Muhammad is to attack their entire life and culture.

Correcting the Misunderstandings
It is wise to find common ground and agree that Muhammad has much in common with Old Testament prophets. Like David and Solomon, he was a political and military leader with multiple wives. Like Moses and Joshua, he united tribes and led them in battle. Like Elijah and many other prophets, he destroyed idols and confronted the corrupt political and economic powers of his day.

Just as Old Testament prophets looked forward to the coming Messiah, Muhammad looked back with respect and admiration to Jesus as the Messiah. The Quran calls *Isa Al Masih* (Jesus) "His (God's) Word" and "a Spirit from Him (God)" (Surah 4:171). It affirms Jesus' virgin birth and special role in the end times, though not in the biblical sense.

Followers of Jesus do not have to insult or embrace Muhammad in order to exalt the Messiah. It is important to lift up Jesus, not tear down Muhammad.

Role of Women

What Muslims Believe

The Perspective of Muslim Women
Muslim women generally consider themselves protected and satisfied within their culture. Their fulfilling social life is usually gender-separated and happens primarily within extended families and some close neighbors.

The Protection of Muslim Women
Women are valued in the Quran. Muhammad brought an end to the practice of female infanticide, widely practiced before his time, and he gave women the right to inherit. The honor of women is a major concern in Muslim societies. The reputation of the family is linked with the women. Islam helps maintain roles and expectations that predate Muhammad. The modest dress code is intended to protect women when outside the home. Muslim women do not need to wear a veil or loose clothes at home or when only women are present.

Polygamy
Since marriage and child bearing are highly valued in Islamic society, polygamy is allowed and yet controlled. Islam limits a man to four wives and requires equal treatment for each.

What Christians Believe

The Perspective of Christian Women
Christians believe that the Bible teaches that both man and woman were created in God's image, had a direct relationship with God, and shared jointly the responsibilities of bringing up children and ruling over the created order (Gen. 1:26–28). Christian husbands and wives are to mutually submit to one another. Women are to respect their husbands; husbands are to sacrificially and selflessly love their wives, just as Jesus Christ loves his church (Eph. 5:21–25).

The Protection of Christian Women
Christian women are to dress modestly (1 Tim. 2:9), and all followers of Jesus are to flee from sexual immorality (1 Cor. 6:18).

Not Conforming to the World
Followers of Jesus believe that they must be transformed by renewing their minds and avoid conforming to the patterns of the secular world (Rom. 12:2). Problems arise when Christians adapt to the Western secular culture more than to the Bible. When this happens there is a decline in morality which leads to an increase in sexual immorality, drunkenness, deceit, selfishness, rage, and other sins.

How to Correct Misunderstandings

The Misunderstandings
Western values conflict with Muslims regarding women perhaps more than any other category. There are several problems in Muslim societies in regard to women. However, secularism and women's liberation have brought the "Christian" West several problems as well.

Correcting the Misunderstandings
Christians, often focused on the plight of Muslim women, fail to see that many Western "solutions" are more to be feared than the problems they address. Many Muslim women prefer their lifestyle to lonely singleness, sexual exploitation, and the desire for money that makes home and family unimportant.

Societies long dominated by Islam have problems which need to be addressed, but before Christians can address these issues they must deal with their own cultural problems. As Jesus said, "You hypocrite, first take the plank out of your own eye, and then you will see clearly to remove the speck from your brother's eye" (Matt. 7:5).

The Do's and Don'ts of Reaching Out to Muslims

Do make it clear you are a follower of Christ, by your loving words and righteous lifestyle.
Don't assume your Muslim friend understands your meaning of "Christian."

Do take time to build a relationship. Practice hospitality.
Don't be surprised if you are rejected at first. It is best to offer Muslim friends store-bought sweets and to avoid anything with pork or alcohol.

Do approach your encounters as a learner. Ask questions.
Don't take notes and treat Muslim friends like an academic project.

Do correct their misunderstandings of your beliefs.
Don't argue. If they want to debate with a Christian, refer them to the website www.debate.org.uk/.

Do talk about Jesus. Use his title, *Isa Al Masih*.
Don't insult the prophet Muhammad.

Do pray out loud with your Muslim friends. Ask if you can pray for their practical needs, healing, and worries. Look for opportunities and pray in Jesus' name.
Don't start your prayer with "Our Father…" because Muslims have a misunderstanding about the fatherhood of God (as sexual). Wait until you correct this misunderstanding before using "Father" or "Abba." At first address your prayer to "Almighty God" or "Lord God."

Do use your right hand in giving and receiving gifts.
Don't use your left hand for eating food (especially when learning to eat with your hands). The left hand is used for toilet cleaning; the right hand for eating.

Do treat your Bible with respect. Store it high on a shelf. Some wrap it in a beautiful cloth.
Don't put your Bible on the floor or in the bathroom as reading material. Many Muslims are superstitious about the bathroom.

Do be gender-sensitive: interact man to man, woman to woman.
Don't allow any compromising situation, even just to protect from a possible rumor. An Arab proverb says, "A man and woman alone together are three with the devil."

Do observe body language. Take your shoes off when entering a home or place of prayer (especially if you see shoes at the threshold).
Don't sit so that the sole of your foot or shoe is facing someone. Women, don't look men directly in the eye, or at least quickly avert your glance.

Do practice modesty, even among Westernized Muslims. For women this is very important since family honor is tied to their behavior and reputation.
Don't assume Muslims think the same as you, even if they dress the same.

ROSE PUBLISHING

Published by Rose Publishing
an imprint of Tyndale House Ministries

rose-publishing.com

Primary author: Rev. Bruce Green, MA, has been building bridges since 1983 between Muslims and a consortium of evangelical churches.

Contributor: Andras Szalai, PhD

Photos/art: Peter Commandeur

Special thanks to: Amal Bejjani, Anne Dinnan (Coordinator of Resource Development Muslim Ministries), and Labib Madanat (Executive Secretary, Palestinian Bible Society)

RELIGION/Christian Theology/Apologetics

ISBN 978-1-89094-767-5

9 781890 947675

461X Islam and Christianity